Eskimos — The Inuit of the Arctic

The Eskimos, or Inuit as they prefer to be known, arrived in Alaska from Asia about 8,000 years ago. Their lives changed very little until the arrival in the Arctic of European adventurers in the sixteenth century. Since then, their culture has suffered a series of major upheavals culminating in the problems of alcoholism, unemployment and depression, which beset them in the 1950s and 60s. Now their position has improved considerably. They run their own schools and businesses and have their own organizations to further their interests. In this book, the author, who works among the Inuit, explains how these changes have come about and tells why the Inuit are looking forward to the future with optimism.

Original Peoples

ESKIMOS
THE INUIT OF THE ARCTIC

J. H. Greg Smith

Rourke Publications, Inc.
Vero Beach, FL 32964

Original Peoples

Eskimos — The Inuit of the Arctic
Aborigines of Australia
Plains Indians of North America
South Pacific Islanders
Indians of the Andes
Zulus of Southern Africa

First published in the
United States in 1987 by
Rourke Publications, Inc.
Vero Beach, FL 32964

Library of Congress Cataloging-in-Publication Data

Smith, J. H. Greg..
  Eskimos : the Inuit of the Arctic.

  (Original peoples)
  Bibliography: p.
  Includes index.
  Summary: Describes the history of the Inuit from
their arrival in Alaska 8,000 years ago to the present
day and discusses the impact of Western influences on
their culture. Includes a glossary of terms.
  1. Eskimos — Juvenile literature. [1. Eskimos]
I. Title. II. Series.
E99.E7S54 1987 970.004'97   87-4331
ISBN 0-086625-257-6

Photoset by Direct Image Photosetting
Printed in Italy by G. Canale & C.S.p.A., Turin

Contents

Introduction

If you had sailed with the Viking Thorfinn Karlsefni on his voyage to the New World in 1003, you would have met with him a race of people he called "Skraelings." This first sighting was typical of many that would follow. A group of small, friendly men dressed in sealskins came paddling out in their sealskin kayaks to meet the visitors. Later these people came to be called Eskimos.

But Eskimos is an outsider's name, which means "eaters of raw flesh." Eskimos themselves prefer to be known simply as *Inuit*, which means "the people" in their own language. For this reason, the name Inuit will be used in this book.

The Inuit live in the Arctic, one of the world's most inhospitable places. Winters are long, dark and cold. Summers are short and plagued by mosquitoes and other insects. The land itself is mostly barren tundra, with few plants or trees. But there is an abundance of wild animals to be taken by the wise and skillful hunter. The Inuit became well adapted to this harsh environment. They built snow-

Many different groups of Inuit live in the Arctic, one of the most inhospitable places on earth.

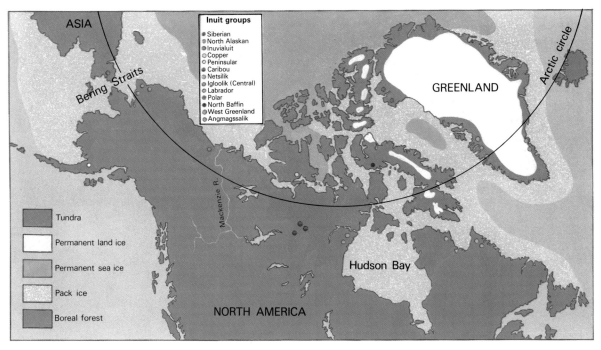

Inuit groups
- Siberian
- North Alaskan
- Inuvialuit
- Copper
- Peninsular
- Caribou
- Netsilik
- Igloolik (Central)
- Labrador
- Polar
- North Baffin
- West Greenland
- Angmagssalik

ASIA

Bering Straits

GREENLAND

Arctic circle

Mackenzie R.

Hudson Bay

NORTH AMERICA

- Tundra
- Permanent land ice
- Permanent sea ice
- Pack ice
- Boreal forest

houses, or *igloos*, for shelter against the coldest winters, and they tamed and harnessed the northern dog. These dogs hauled food, tents, skins and other necessities on *komatiks* — supple wooden sleds.

Life in the Arctic was hard, and it remains so. But the barren landscape has changed its image. The north has become a potential source of great wealth from oil, gas and minerals.

The Arctic region is covered by snow for most of the year.

The Inuit too are changing. The igloo is largely a house of the past and dog teams have largely given way to motorized sleds, called *skidoos*. This book tells the story of the Inuit — their history, their life-style today, and their future in the modern world.

Chapter 1 **By Land and Sea from Asia**

The Earliest Inuit

The ancestors of today's Inuit came from Asia. They crossed the Bering Strait into what is now Alaska about 8,000 years ago, using the two islands of Big and Little Diomede as stepping stones. Four thousand years later, they had ranged as far eastward as Greenland. Like the Inuit of more modern times, they hunted or fished for their food. But they had not yet invented the *kayak* to help them in their pursuit of fish and sea mammals. These were first used by a group of people who lived in the Cape Dorset region of Baffin Island around 800 B.C.

These people are known as the Dorset culture. They were nomads, who hunted seals, walrus and caribou. As well as inventing the

The ancestors of today's Inuit crossed the Bering Strait from Asia into what is now North America about 8,000 years ago.

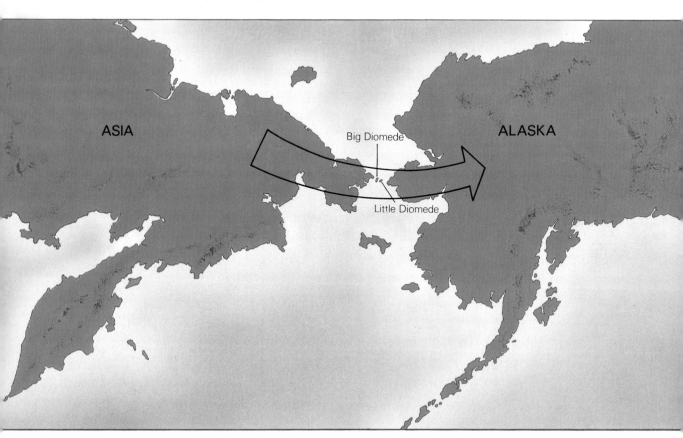

A bone comb with an archer engraved on it. This was made by a member of the Dorset culture in about 500 B.C.

kayak, they may also have been the first people to make igloos. The Dorsets probably lived in skin tents in summer. In the cold winter, they dug pits, which they roofed over with skins. These underground homes they lit and heated with lamps, called *kudliks*, in which they burned seal oil.

The Dorset culture lasted for nearly 2,000 years, eventually occupying an area stretching from Greenland in the east to the Mackenzie Delta in the west, and as far south as Newfoundland and Labrador.

The decline of the Dorset culture was brought about, in part at least, by a change in the weather. Between A.D. 800 and 1300, the climate became much warmer in the north. This meant that people could live more settled lives and did not need to be nomads. One such group of settled people were the Thule.

9

The Thule

The Thule were a small, hardy and clever people who probably originated in the region of Alaska about A.D. 900. Using dog teams, they rapidly spread eastward. Within 300 years, they had replaced the Dorsets, either by wiping them out, or by absorbing them into their own culture.

The Thule not only hunted caribou, seals, walrus and fish, but had also developed the means of killing the giant bowhead whales. With great daring, the Thule hunters would put out to sea in kayaks and the larger *umiaks* — wooden-framed boats covered with sealskin.

The Thule were probably the first people to use dogs to pull their sleds.

The advantage of being able to hunt these sixty-foot (eighteen-meter) mammals was that one whale could supply as much blubber as 1,000 seals. So the Thule were relatively rich. The ready supply of food and fuel meant that they could live in large, more permanent communities of up to thirty-five houses. These houses were usually dug into hillsides along the coast. The walls were of stone, and whalebones were used to make rafters for the roof. These were all covered with turfs. Inside, flat stones were used to line the floors and to build sleeping platforms and cupboards.

Once more, however, nature intervened. Around the seventeenth century, it became much colder in the north. Ice blocked the open water where the Thule hunted whales. Summers became shorter, and food and fuel more scarce. So the Thule were forced to split into smaller groups and return to a nomadic life.

These changes led to the development of modern Inuit culture. Small groups of people began to range across the Arctic from Siberia to eastern Greenland. By the eighteenth century the Thule had been almost completely replaced by these nomadic people and only a few scattered communities of permanent homes remained.

Using large boats, called umiaks, the Thule hunters were able to chase the giant bowhead whales.

Chapter 2 **Life with the Inuit**

Winter and Spring Hunting

The Inuit were always on the move, journeying along the coast in pursuit of the animals that provided food, clothing, tools, fuel and shelter. During the cold winters, which could last up to ten months, the Inuit traveled mostly by dog team and sometimes on foot. They made camps on the sea ice, where they could find the seals that formed their staple diet. Often a patient hunter would wait for two days for a seal to surface at a breathing hole. Then he would have to react very quickly to spear it with his harpoon. Back at camp, the seals would be quickly skinned and cut up by the women, using sharp knives called *ulus*. Then the pieces of meat would be shared out equally.

Everything an Inuit family needed to survive the winter would be carried on a sled. These possessions could include seal and caribou skins for tents and bedding, lances and harpoons, harpoon lines, lamps and pots, implements and tools for repairing the sled, a roll of dried

An Inuit family had to carry everything it needed on its sled.

grass for lining the boots, some dried moss for a lamp wick and a few small pieces of walrus meat or blubber for food.

Toward March, the days became longer and the spring hunting period would begin. The days, though perhaps as cold as minus 40°F (−40°C), were often blessed with sunshine, which brought the seals out onto the ice.

Polar bears also live on seals, and occasionally an Inuit hunter came across one. With his dogs, he would track the bear until it was cornered. Then he would close in with his spear for the kill. Killing a bear, one of the most dangerous of animals, was a sign of manhood and a cause for celebration. A single animal

An Inuit hunter would often have to travel many miles across the ice in search of his prey.

could provide many days' food, and the skin could be used to make warm, waterproof clothing.

Summer Camps

When the spring ice became too weak, the Inuit moved onto the land, camping in tents along the shore. When open water reappeared, kayaks could be used to hunt seals and whales, and the larger umiaks were loaded up and used for traveling. Summer camps were happy places. By June and July the Arctic wildlife had returned from its migrations and the warm burrows of winter.

Fish could be taken with hooks, nets and spears, and game was plentiful. Life became easier for a few months.

There were foxes to be caught in stone traps, and more than enough birds, squirrels, Arctic hares, seals, whales, walrus, narwhal, muskrats, musk ox or caribou, depending upon location. The Arctic vegetation came alive, providing a ready supply of favorite plants, such as sorrel and angelica, and many kinds of berries.

Once the ice on the seas and lakes had melted, the Inuit could take to the water in search of seals.

Musk ox were a prime source of meat for the Inuit during the summer months.

But these plants were just a delicacy, for the Inuit could get all the vitamins they needed by eating raw certain parts of the animals they caught.

Much of the summer's work was concerned with preparing for the next winter. As always, children helped with the many chores, learning by watching their parents. Fish had to be caught and smoked or dried. Meat, too, was dried, and caches made in the permafrost where it could be stored for use in winter.

15

Social Life

When Inuit groups met on the land or at summer or winter camps, they made the time fly with feasts, drum dancing and games. Stories were told, and legends handed down from generation to generation. The Inuit had many pastimes to help amuse themselves. String games, rather like cat's cradle, were used to illustrate stories. Another game used a piece of bone pierced with several holes. It was joined by a string to a stick. The player had to flip the bone so that it landed with the stick in one of the holes.

A popular game at summer camps was the one shown here. The men in the background are playing the finger pull game.

The Inuit also enjoyed good-natured competitions such as foot races and wrestling matches. Especially fun was the blanket toss, and the ear pull, mouth pull and finger pull made for much laughter.

As with the rest of Inuit life, everyone took part in these activities. Adults were not separated from children, or men from women. There were no formal leaders. Elders were respected for their wisdom and experience, individual men for their ability as hunters, and *shamans* for their magical and spiritual powers. Children were especially loved and treated with great affection.

The Inuit were concerned with the good of the whole group. The harshness of their lives sometimes led to practices we might find hard to understand. Female babies might be left to die if a family decided there were too many mouths to feed. In times of starvation, elders might walk off into the snow to die in order that others might live. Such actions resulted from a need to make very difficult choices at times. Yet the Inuit remained remarkably cheerful and optimistic. Arguments and squabbles were rare. Although the Inuit language had over seventy words for snow, there wasn't a single word for war.

Births, deaths and marriages were all treated as special occasions and certain rituals had to be observed. Special amulets were given to newborn babies to give them skill in hunting or sewing. When someone died they were left in their homes for four days. Then they were dressed in their best clothes, wrapped in furs and taken to a special place. There they were left on the snow or ice for animals to eat. The Inuit believed that this helped to release the spirit.

Inuit marriages were usually arranged by parents. An Inuit man usually spent up to a year living with his fiancee's parents so that the two people and their families could get to know each other. As well as their husbands or wives, people often had relationships with other men or women. These were called "exchange marriages." If a woman's husband died, which happened quite often in the dangerous Arctic, she could rely on her exchange husband for support.

The summer camp was a place for swapping stories, playing games, carving ornaments or repairing weapons.

Chapter 3   **The Europeans Come**

The Search for the Northwest Passage

The Norsemen of Scandinavia were the first Europeans to journey and settle in the Arctic regions. Although their relationship with the "Skraelings," as they called the people of Greenland, was often unfriendly, they had little effect upon the Inuit way of life, and by 1500 most of their colonies had disappeared.

Around this time, however, it became widely believed in Europe that a passage existed across the north of Canada that ships could use as a short cut to sail to the Far East and China to trade for spices. The captain who found the passage would earn fame and fortune.

An Englishman, Martin Frobisher, led the first major expedition to search for the Northwest Passage. This ship, the Gabriel, arrived in what is now Frobisher Bay on Baffin Island in the summer of 1576. Frobisher was the first Englishman known to have met the Inuit.

At about the same time the search for the Passsage brought explorers into contact with the Inuit of Greenland. In 1605 another Englishman, James Hall, was sent to Greenland by Danish employers to look for silver.

However, these early encounters between Englishmen and Inuit often ended in tragedy. Inuit were killed or captured and brought back to Europe where they were put on exhibition like zoo animals; most died soon after reaching their new homes.

An early Norse settlement in Greenland.

Frobisher and his men under attack from a group of hostile Inuit.

Below *The search for the Northwest Passage took many ships to hitherto unexplored regions.*

Frobisher and Hall were followed by many other explorers. Hundreds of men would die of cold, scurvy and starvation looking for the Northwest Passage. An entire expedition, led by Sir John Franklin, disappeared in 1847 with 129 men lost to the Arctic winter. But gradually, as ships began to overwinter in the north, the explorers learned the Inuit techniques of survival. Once they did so, they started to use many of their tricks themselves.

Fur Traders and Whalers

It was not only the search for the Northwest Passage that brought Europeans into contact with the Inuit. By the seventeenth century, fur was increasingly in demand and companies that received trading rights set up posts throughout the north.

The Danish government gave all trading rights to the Royal Greenland Trading Company. Until 1953, this was the only company allowed to trade with Greenland. Meanwhile in Canada, the Hudson's Bay Company was given nearly 1½ million square miles (4 million square kilometers) of land by King Charles II of Britain. By 1821, it controlled or owned half the country,

A Hudson's Bay Company trading post in Canada in 1849.

but sold its title a few years later to the Dominion of Canada.

Both these companies possessed great power over the regions they controlled and the people who lived there. If an *Inuk* did not want to trade on their terms it was too bad. He had nowhere else to go. Many Inuit became dependent upon these companies for their livelihoods.

Similarly in Alaska, which was then part of the Russian Empire, fur traders interrupted the peaceful life of the native peoples. Most of the Aleuts, cousins of the Inuit, were either killed or made slaves. During the eighteenth century, their numbers dropped from twenty thousand to two thousand in just a few years. Eventually, however, the Russians gave up Alaska without settling there permanently.

Of all the newcomers to the north, the whalers had the greatest impact on the Inuit. Each year, hundreds of boats set out in search of the giant bowhead whale that provided oil and baleen — whalebone that was used to make ladies' corsets.

The whalers were often rough, greedy men who cared little for the native people they met. They wiped out the sea mammals and other wildlife upon which the Inuit depended. They brought diseases, alcohol and violence.

At the same time, the Inuit came to rely on the whalers for trade and for part-time jobs. When the whaling industry collapsed around 1912, the massacre of wildlife made it hard for the Inuit to return to their old ways of life.

Whalers, hunting in ships like this one, often played havoc with the Inuit people.

The Missionaries

The Inuit were also visited by missionaries. Many ended up spending their lives in the north. The first to visit Greenland was a Lutheran minister, Hans P. Egede, who was determined to find the last of the Norse colonists and convert them and the Inuit to Christianity. Although he did not find any Norse

Inuit at prayer in a modern church in Greenland.

descendants, he did write one of the first detailed accounts of Inuit life, and did much to encourage understanding of the Inuit.

In Labrador the Moravians set up missions in the mid-eighteenth century. They helped to make peace between Indians and Inuit, and by 1850 most Inuit had been converted to their church. For the next 100 years the Moravians controlled trade in the region. But, although well-intentioned, they often treated the Inuit like children.

By around 1925, Catholic, Anglican and Protestant missionaries had entered the Arctic. They eventually converted many of the Inuit, and held a firm place in their lives. Their work had both good and bad results. They gave medical help to the Inuit, saved many dialects by writing them down, and discouraged violence and

The missionaries were the first to give the Inuit languages a written form.

alcoholism. On the other hand, they often upset traditional life by insisting that men take only one wife, by banning shamans and forbidding drum dances. While they helped to educate Inuit children, they did so in mission schools where they were not allowed to speak their own language, and where their customs were not taught. This cut off many children from their parents. Yet many Inuit today remain attached to the priests and missionaries who live among them.

An attempt to blend Inuit style with Christianity is this Igloo Church in Inuvik, in Canada.

The Twentieth Century

After the hard times following the departure of the whalers, there was a boom in fur prices during the 1920s. Many Inuit turned to trapping and trading. But when the boom ended in the thirties, many starved. Even as late as the 1950s, it was not uncommon for Inuit to die of starvation.

The epidemics brought by the white man continued. By 1950, one in five Inuit had tuberculosis. These were the survivors. Many thousands had died already from diphtheria, measles and influenza.

World War II brought fears of invasion through the north by Japanese or Germans. Greater interest was taken in the region and much knowledge was gained as a result. After the war, the tensions between the Russians and the Americans led to further developments. In the 1950s, a line of radar stations, the Distant Early Warning (DEW) Line, was set up. It stretched from Alaska to eastern Canada. The construction of the DEW Line gave jobs to many Inuit. Often they gave up their lives on the land as hunters and trappers to settle near the sta-

An Inuit graveyard in the western Arctic. The epidemics of the nineteenth and early twentieth centuries ravaged the Inuit population.

The construction of the DEW Line across North America in the 1950s brought many Inuit into permanent settlements.

tions. Imagine their surprise when they learned a few years later that they were no longer needed. The stations were all to be run by non-Inuit technicians. The sudden loss of jobs turned many Inuit toward welfare and handouts.

Around the same time, the Russians were turning their attention toward their polar regions. They removed the last of their Inuit from the Diomede Islands in the Bering Strait, and contact between them and other Inuit was virtually cut off.

Chapter 4   The Search for an Inuit Voice

The Rush to Modernize

By the 1950s and 60s, people throughout the world were beginning to show concern over the plight of the Inuit. They were shocked by the disease, starvation and alcoholism. In Canada, Alaska and Greenland, huge bureaucracies were developed to deal with native problems. At the same time, the period brought a push from outside to modernize and develop the north.

Without asking the Inuit them-

This is typical of the Inuit homes that were constructed by the Canadian government in the 1960s and 70s.

selves, outsiders began making decisions about their lives. Wherever the Inuit lived, they were invaded by bureaucrats, teachers, "experts," scientists, administrators and businessmen. The Inuit were moved often hundreds of miles into permanent communities where they had access to schools, hospitals and other services. Sometimes the locations were totally unsuitable. Because there were no animals to hunt, the Inuit would starve, or end up having to move back to their old homes. Often, they were encouraged to start up businesses, many of which foundered.

In the 1950s and 60s many attempts were made to bring the Inuit together into permanent communities.

In each case, the result was the same — a total upheaval. Inuit culture has never valued personal ambition, collecting possessions, or breaking up of families or friendships just to get ahead. The well-being of the community was what counted most. A hunter's life depended upon nature's time, not the clock. If a man had to wait by a seal's breathing hole for two days, he did so. If a family could not travel for a week because of a storm, they waited. Trying to fit these attitudes into a nine-to-five routine caused great unhappiness for many Inuit.

27

Educational Problems

In Greenland, Inuit children were taught by Danish teachers in Danish, rather than their own Greenlandic language. In Canada and Alaska, non-Inuit teachers taught children in English. Many children were brought from their communities to stay in dormitories far from home. The texts they studied were usually the same as those used by children in other parts of Canada and the U.S. They talked more often about farms, cars and suburbs than about northern subjects.

In the 1950s and 60s Inuit children were taught in English or Danish and not in their native languages.

Many Inuit who went through these systems in the 1950s and 1960s found themselves cut off from their own way of life, their families and their culture. They had never learned the skills needed for hunting, fishing and trapping. Sometimes parents and children could no longer even talk together in the same language. At the same time they were not comfortable in the white person's world.

The result was an increase in discipline problems, a turning away from the old ways, and growing use of drugs and alcohol. Because there were often no jobs for these newly educated young people, many were forced into depending on welfare. All of this caused much bitterness.

By the 1960s, Inuit in all three countries felt growing frustration. Their culture was being taken away; their children turned into strangers; and their lives controlled by others. The Inuit started to look for ways to take back responsibility for their own affairs.

A town school in Greenland in 1962. Schoolchildren were often removed from their parents to live in school dormitories.

The Inuit fear that oil exploration in the Arctic will pollute the sea and destroy the animals on which they depend.

The planned construction of the Alaska pipeline in the 1970s prompted many Alaskans to press for settlement of their land claims.

Oil and Gas Discoveries

In 1968, large amounts of oil and gas were discovered off the coast of Alaska. Suddenly the pace of development became frantic. Pressure on the Inuit and their homeland increased. To them, it seemed that industry and governments could only see the profits to be made from shipping oil and gas out of the north. The Inuit began to fear that wildlife would disappear and the land and sea become polluted. If they did not take action they would soon have no voice in their own land.

The Inuit began to organize. Across the Arctic their arguments were the same. They wanted their traditional rights to the land recognized. They wanted the Arctic nature and wildlife protected. And above all, they wanted more say in running their own lives.

In Canada they were successful in stopping a pipeline down the Mackenzie Valley to the Beaufort Sea. They wanted big projects such as this to be more carefully thought out. What would be the effect upon the caribou herds? How would any oil spills be cleaned up? How would it change people's lives in the communities along its path? These and other important issues had to be looked at before construction began.

North American Land Claims

The Inuit did not believe in signing land treaties with governments. In their view no English king or Russian czar could hand over Inuit lands to someone else. Therefore, the land was still theirs. They wanted their governments to sign agreements with them which would recognize this, and protect them and their land. At the same time, they hoped that such agreements would give them a share in any benefits from development.

In Alaska such an agreement was signed into law by the United States Congress in 1971. The Alaska Native Claims Settlement awarded 44 million acres (17,800,000 hectares) of land and over 900 million dollars to the Aleuts, Indians and Inuit of Alaska. With this money as a base, corporations were set up to start businesses and give opportunities to the native people for jobs and training. These businesses are owned and controlled by the native people themselves. They also got the right to run many of their own local affairs through regional governments.

Inuit leaders of the western Arctic meet to discuss strategy and local affairs.

In Canada only one such agreement has been signed, at James Bay in northern Quebec in 1975. Others seem to be getting closer, and the Inuit may have such agreements in place within a couple of years.

The Inuit of Canada are also trying to establish their own territory in the north. To be called *Nunavut* ("our land"), this territory would give the Inuit greater control over their own affairs. While still a part of

A meeting between Inuit leaders and representatives of an oil company. Although interested in the benefits of development, many Inuit are worried by its side effects.

Canada, Nunavut would reflect Inuit culture and language. In 1982, residents of the Canadian north voted in favor of creating Nunavut. Political leaders are now working out the details of how Nunavut is to be set up.

Greenland Home Rule

The search for an Inuit voice has led to the rise of Inuit political movements, which promote the interests of their people. In the 1970s, the Greenlanders expressed their feelings to the Danish government. They were unhappy at being governed from abroad, at being paid less than Danes in their own country, and at an educational system that was not in their own language. Above all, they did not want to be forced to give up their traditional hunting life, which was the root of Inuit culture.

These new Greenland voices were eventually heard in Denmark and by 1979 Greenland had won home rule. Under home rule, Greenland remains part of Denmark, but has the power to elect its own officials and to run many of its own affairs. Culture, language, education, and economic and social affairs are all run by the Greenlanders themselves.

Nuuk, in Greenland, is the capital of that country and the seat of the home rule government.

The Inuit Circumpolar Conference

Above *Jonathan Motzfeldt (center) is Greenland's first home rule premier.*

In Alaska, Canada and Greenland, the Inuit now have their own newspapers, radio and television programs, and political organizations to represent their views. It was only natural that they should try to find a way to present their views to the outside world as well.

In 1977, at a historic meeting in Barrow, Alaska, an organization was formed that would represent all Inuit. The Inuit Circumpolar Conference was set up to defend Inuit culture and language, and the Arctic nature and wildlife. It has met twice since then, once in Greenland in 1980 and again in Canada in 1983. In 1983 the I.C.C. was granted recognition by the United Nations.

The general assembly of the Inuit Circumpolar Conference in session.

Chapter 5 **The Inuit Today**

The modern Inuit child is probably as happy playing with videos as the more traditional games.

The Modern Inuit World

The Inuit today live in a very different world from that of even twenty-five years ago. Many changes have come to the north. Now, the "average" Inuit family probably lives in a permanent wooden house. This house might have central heating, and a bathroom and built-in kitchen with a stove and refrigerator. In the living room there might be a television, radio and stereo, and perhaps a video-cassette recorder.

Modern technology links many communities to the outside world through satellite television, and video-cassettes can be rented to watch the latest films. Through high-frequency radio, hunters and trappers can remain in touch with their home base and each other while out on the land.

Snowmobiles, or skidoos, have largely replaced the traditional dog teams, and boats used in the summer are equipped with motors. Most communities have a regular air service. This mobility has given many Inuit access to services and goods from the outside world. They can also visit each other, despite the great distances in the north. For many Inuit, taking an airplane is as common as riding on a bus is for most of us. The airplane has also assisted the Inuit political movements, for now they can easily meet together with Inuit from other regions. For example, there are two flights a week between Nuuk, the capital of Greenland, and Frobisher Bay in Canada.

Technology has brought the modern world closer to many Inuit. Even in the most remote areas they now have access to air transportation, radio and television.

The Schools

Even the smallest Inuit community usually has its own school and health clinic, and a store where people can buy canned foods, tools, clothes and other articles. The schools have changed too. Although many teachers still come from outside the north, the educational system is becoming more sensitive to Inuit culture. More and more schools teach the Inuit language. Inuit stories, legends, hunting, trapping or other traditional activities are taught.

The school year is usually timed so the children can go spring hunting

Nowadays, Inuit children are sometimes taught by Inuit teachers in their own language.

or summer fishing with their parents. Most Inuit families still get most of their food from the land. If you were an Inuit child, you would welcome these trips with your parents and family. You might find yourself racing along on a sunny spring day, your skidoo pulling a komatik, in search of caribou. If the hunt were successful, you would help to load the animal and bring it home.

You might camp at a lake with

your family for a week to catch fat trout or char, or go out in a boat with your father in summer to hunt for seals. You would look forward to the excitement and freedom of these trips and your time on the land would be as important to your education as your time at school.

Inuit children are expected to help out with the hunting as well as attend school.

A Foot in Two Worlds

In larger towns, however, many Inuit do not have the chance to hunt and fish as do those in smaller communities. They are as likely to amuse themselves at rock dances as by hunting. Like their parents, these young Inuit often live with a foot in two worlds.

Clothing styles are an example of the mix of old and new cultures. If you were an Inuk, your jeans, shirt and sweater would have been bought in a store. In winter, they would be covered by a handmade parka. You might wear moosehide *mukluks* trimmed with seal, caribou or musk ox fur. Your mitts would be big enough to come up over your sleeves and would be trimmed with wolf, fox or bear fur.

This mixture of products from the land with those made elsewhere and bought from stores means that the Inuit must know, not just how to hunt and fish, but also how to earn cash. This money can come from selling their arts and crafts, furs, meat and fish, or by working for wages. The Inuit find positions in government, with oil companies, fish plants and other enterprises. Some Inuit work for their own organizations, which are busy investing in hotels, mines, seafood companies, fisheries, ships and airlines. The Inuit, remembering the slump in whaling and the fur trade, want to build businesses that will last. By

also investing in guiding, tourism and the sale of country foods such as fish and caribou, they know they will keep their traditional skills even if world markets change. Despite these advances, lack of employment still remains a serious problem in many Inuit communities.

Today, many Inuit own and work in co-operative businesses.

40

The Inuit today are both modern and traditional at the same time. Here a family cuts steaks from an Arctic char they have just caught. Their skidoo requires cash to purchase and maintain.

41

Games like seal skinning (above) and blanket tossing (below) keep traditions alive and help pass them on to young Inuit.

Back to the Land

The feeling of being cut off from their culture has encouraged many young Inuit to discover more about the old ways. There is renewed pride in Inuit culture. Many Inuit are working on projects to record legends, history and life stories from the past. The skills of camping, hunting and trapping are being taught to the young, and children are being encouraged to learn the language of their parents. Dog teams are being used once more and traditional sporting competitions, such as the Northern Games, are being organized. These include events like the blanket toss, one-foot high kick, seal skinning and tea boiling contests. Modern rock dances are held, but so too are old-time dances, where jigs, square dances and drum dances are popular.

Family ties remain strong among the Inuit. One of the hardest things a young person can do is to leave his or her home community to take up a job or go to school outside. Homesickness is often a problem and very few Inuit live outside the Arctic for that very reason.

There are still difficulties, of course. Sometimes people turn to alcohol, and this is one of the biggest problems in the north. Alcohol abuse disrupts family life, and leads to poor health, violence, sometimes death from freezing in the winter, and often dependence on welfare or other government aid. Services in the north have greatly improved but there are still too few Inuit doctors, dentists, teachers, lawyers and other professionals.

Yet most Inuit are optimistic. They are at last gaining control over their own lives. Their standard of living is constantly improving and the epidemics that killed so many in the past have been brought under control. The Inuit look forward to a bright future, but, as the next chapter shows, that future will not be without problems of its own.

Hunting for food is still an important part of the Inuit way of life.

43

Chapter 6 **The Inuit Future**

The success of the Inuit movement in the last fifteen years has shown that the Inuit are in the north to stay. It is their homeland and the source of their culture. Yet the north is under attack from several directions. In Europe and elsewhere violent opposition to seal hunting and the fur trade in general is a serious threat. Already fur prices have dropped, reducing Inuit income.

Inuit still sometimes use sleds and dogs for transportation . . .

Although they do not oppose development, the Inuit are worried about some of its effects. The land and sea, and the animals that live there, are vitally important. The Inuit fear that too urgent a rush to develop the north will be dangerous for its lands and its wildlife. They know that, long after the oil companies have gone, *they* will remain.

The Inuit future is also at risk from modern technology. The airplane, radio, television and other such things are widely used by the

. . . but airplanes and helicopters bring them into contact with outside influences that endanger their culture.

Inuit. But they bring them into contact with outside influences. Inuit children watch the same television programs as children in the south or in Europe. In regions of the north where non-Inuit come to live and work, Inuit culture often takes second place to that of the new residents. These two influences may result in a gradual loss of Inuit language and culture unless the Inuit themselves are successful in saving them.

The Inuit have made great advances in the past few years, and are generally optimistic about their future. But they know that the fight to preserve their culture and the northern environment upon which it depends is far from over.

Glossary

Angelica A plant with small white or greenish flowers. Its seeds, leaves and stems are used in medicine and cookery.

Baleen Whalebone. The baleen, which grows inside the mouth of the bowhead whale, was once used to make ladies' corsets.

Blanket toss A game often played when many Inuit get together. The edges of a skin blanket are held by as many people as possible. One person stands on the blanket itself. By pulling simultaneously on the edges of the blanket a trampoline effect is created and the person can be thrown high into the air. Points are awarded on the basis of acrobatic skill, balance and style.

Blubber The fat of whales or other sea mammals.

Breathing hole A hole in the ice through which sea mammals like the seal come up to breathe.

Cache A hidden store of food.

Caribou A large deer that lives in the Arctic regions of North America.

Char A trout-like fish that lives in cold lakes and northern seas.

Dialect A way of speaking used in a particular part of a country or by a particular group of people.

Diphtheria An infectious disease of the throat.

Drum dance An Inuit form of entertainment and cultural expression. Men would beat on skin drums while both men and women danced. Each man had his own song, which no one else could sing. As the beat accelerated the dancers' movements kept pace. Songs and dances were accompanied by the stamping of feet in time with the drum beat.

Ear pull A game in which two men sat close together and facing one another. Each hooked a thong around the other's ear or ears. Then they leaned back and pulled. The first to give in lost.

Epidemic An outbreak of a disease that spreads and affects a lot of people.

Foot races Running races.

Home rule Government of a country by the people who live there and not by another country.

Lutheran A member of the Lutheran Church. This is a church founded by Martin Luther in the sixteenth century.

Moravian A member of the Moravian Church, a church founded in Moravia (now Czechoslovakia) in the eighteenth century.

Mouth pull A game in which two men stand side by side and pass a hand around each other's neck until they could hook a finger into each other's mouth. At a signal they would pull on the inside cheek until one or other gave in.

Nomad A member of a group of people who have no fixed home and who wander from place to place.

Norseman A person from ancient Scandinavia (now Sweden, Norway, Denmark and Finland).

One-foot high kick A game in which an athlete has to kick a high object with one foot and then land back on the same foot. Good athletes can kick up to about eight feet.

Permafrost Ground that is permanently frozen.

Sorrel A plant of the north that can be used in sauces.

Tuberculosis An infectious disease of the lungs.

Tundra The cold, treeless region of the northern Arctic.

Glossary of Inuit Words

Eskimo Actually an Indian word, it means "eaters of raw flesh." Although unflattering, it came into wide use, even among those it described.

Igloo (Also spelled Iglu.) The dome-shaped snowhouse of the Inuit.

Inuit "The people" in their own language. This is the name by which the Inuit prefer to be known. It is quickly replacing the word Eskimo.

Inuk One Inuit person.

Kayak (Also spelled Qayaq.) The slender, sealskin-covered boat of the Inuit.

Komatik The Inuit sled. Long and supple, komatiks were pulled by dog teams. Today they are still widely used, and often pulled by skidoos.

Kudlik (Also spelled Qulliq.) The traditional soapstone lamp. It burned whale oil or seal oil and used a moss wick. Kudliks were used for cooking, heating and light.

Mukluk The Inuit boot. Made from sealskin, caribou, or other fur, mukluks usually had moosehide or sealskin soles. Lined with moss, they were surprisingly warm. Today felt is used instead of moss.

Nunavut An Inuit word meaning "our land." It is the name of the new territory in northern Canada which, when it is formed, will reflect Inuit culture and language.

Shamans Inuit men and women who had spiritual, almost magical powers. They used these powers to cure sickness and communicate with the spirits to help their people. Wise shamans were usually recognized as leaders.

Ulu A crescent-shaped knife, traditionally used by Inuit women.

Books to Read

Some of the books listed here may no longer be in print but should still be available in libraries.

An Eskimo Family by Bryan and Cherry Alexander (Lerner, 1985).

Eskimos by Kaj Birket-Smith (Crown, 1971).

People of the Ice Whale by David Boeri (Dutton, 1983).

Eskimos by Mary Bringle (Watts, 1973).

Eskimos by Derek Fordham (Silver, 1979).

Eskimos by Jill Hughes (Watts, 1984).

Eskimos by Fred L. Israel (Chelsea House, 1987).

The Northwest Passage by Bern Keating (Rand, McNalley, 1977).

Eskimos by Carolyn Meyer (Atheneum, 1977).

People of the Deer by Farley Mowat (Little, Brown, 1952).

Shadow of the Hunter: Stories of Eskimo Life by Richard K. Nelson (University of Chicago Press, 1980).

The Eskimo: The Inuit and Yupik People by Alice Osinski (Childrens Press, 1985).

Dogsong by Gary Paulsen (Bradbury, 1985).

Eskimos by Susan Purdy and Cass R. Sandak (Watts, 1982).

In the Middle: The Eskimo Today by Stephen G. Williams (Godine, 1983).

© Copyright 1984 by Wayland (Publishers) Limited
61 Western Road, Hove, East Sussex BN3 lJD, England

Index